Alpha Ruins

The Bucknell Series in Contemporary Poetry

This is one of a limited number of books of poetry of the
highest quality published annually by the Bucknell University
Press, in conjunction with *West Branch Literary Journal* and
the Stadler Center for Poetry.

Titles in This Series

Karl Patten, *Touch*
Afaa Weaver, *The Ten Lights of God*
Charles Borkhuis, *Alpha Ruins*

http://www.departments.bucknell.edu/univ_press

Alpha Ruins

Charles Borkhuis

Lewisburg
Bucknell University Press
London: Associated University Presses

Associated University Presses
440 Forsgate Drive
Cranbury, NJ 08512

Associated University Presses
16 Barter Street
London WC1A 2AH, England

Associated University Presses
P.O. Box 338, Port Credit
Mississauga, Ontario
Canada L5G 4L8

The paper used in this publication meets the requirements of the American National Standard for Permanence of Paper for Printed Library Materials Z39.48-1984.

Library of Congress Cataloging-in-Publication Data

Borkhuis, Charles.
    Alpha Ruins
        p.   cm.—(The Bucknell series in contemporary poetry)
    ISBN 0-8387-5442-2 (alk. paper)
    I. Series.
    PS3552.O7538 A79   2000
    811'.54—dc21   99-054645

Other books by Charles Borkhuis

Poetry
  Hypnogogic Sonnets—1992
  Proximity (Stolen Arrows)—1995
  Dinner with Franz—1998

Plays
  Poet's Theater: An Anthology—1981
    Phantom Limbs
  Sunspots—1993
  Mouth of Shadows: Two Plays—1999
    Hamlet's Ghosts Perform Hamlet
    Sunspots

for Kathleen

Contents

IV

V

Acknowledgments

The author gratefully acknowledges the following publications in which poems in *Alpha Ruins* first appeared:

Situation: "Alpha Ruins"
New American Writing: "Pebbles in the Mouth"
Talisman: "Touch My Money and Leave," "Severed Moon"
First Intensity: "Farther," "Glass River Divide," "The Rapture," "Dream of the Everyday World," "Hauling Light Home in a Box"
Orpheus Grid: "On the Periphery," "Nobody"
Five Fingers: "Blank Page Already Black"
Tool: "Sight Lines," "The Gaze," "Marginalia"
Poetry New York: "Write What I say," "Deader Than Dead," "Fractal Geometry"
Lingo: "Close Up and Far Away"
Avec: "The Surgeon's Glove"
American Letters and Commentary: "Transparencies"
Phoebe: "Little Numbers," "That"
Kiosk: "Empty When We Look"
Heavenbone: "Orpheus Dividing"
The Little Magazine (CD-ROM): "State of Mind"
The World: "Second Sight"
Yefief: "Eye to Eye"
Exquisite Corpse: "Acquired Characteristics"

Anthologies:

The Gertrude Stein Awards in Innovative Poetry (1995–1996) "Farther"
O.blēk: Writing from the New Coast: "Slice of Life"
The Avec Sampler Two: "The French Disease," "Intimacy," "The Mirror and It's Double," "Code Heroes"

Alpha Ruins

I

lets us
begin where I must

from the failure of systems

—Robert Duncan
After a Long Illness

Alpha Ruins

enter anywhere

first and last
drifting toward the same
moving empty center

decomposition clocked
loop of talking minutes
ripened fruit
buried in the spot
on her hand

inside a guarded premise
the night unfolds its chairs
opens a crumbling mouth

a falling away
in parallel rotation

gesture of mind
if mercury then lead

what observes creates
caught in the materials
in a bird's beak
where I wriggle

bones break into words
the skin is a sticky gum
for blowing bubbles

"I" is just another letter
a candle burning in the mirror

as if someone had planted
snails in my face

as if bending at the knee
I will see
my own small town
in the detritus and dust

Pebbles in the Mouth

knowing less what was meant
but in the saying
what is released what travels
within the sound of meaning's slide
over the loose rocks
of metaphor and mimesis

between anticipation and memory
something drops like a pebble
something in the telling twisted
inescapably altered by the word *pebble*
that opens onto a chaos of incomparable energy

void without distinction
through which the poem passes
beyond the blades of division
the emptiness is immense
and deep with indifference
silence doesn't need you
but you've found it

and lost it
and now can't will it back
hence the small terrors return
as death's new sentence
jumps off the shapes of chairs and forks
tables and people like little flames of fear
or sorrow attached to the edges of this world
attached to words sewn through the world
that mean something but not enough
to keep the nothing out

Touch My Money and Leave

"I'm still big. It's the pictures that got small."

—Norma Desmond
Sunset Boulevard

where limits equal
one bacon burger sunset

hope in an air pump
the sign said SALVATION
twelve miles ahead

twenty painters painting
a football field sky
that is sunny all day

at home in the homily
let me lie down drunk
on your recalcitrant lawn
after its hundred beheadings

let me place my own head
between the blades of morning
and imagine a brown cow
on a white milk carton
mooing to me personally . . .

~

"drink miss?" the butler smiles
while grinding his teeth"

(most cold-blooded murderers prefer milk)

"eros is sick"
says the card addressed to me
it is signed "an admirer"

I become a fetish-object
dancing under bright lights
get up and grind laugh
show teeth tits turn

get pissed make a scene
make an impression
cash-in on the fall out

write a book give interviews
make a movie play myself
sell options produce photo ops
become a drug addict
lose money friends and teeth
go to rehab act out psycho-dramas

wind up wrestling on the couch
with the rapist
"that's ah . . . therapist to you"

I want to grab a gun and shoot
into a crowded street of therapists
but of course it's been done

even to become
the first mailwoman to go postal
is not fresh enough

"who's fucking language is this anyway?"

"why don't you take another pill?"

~

the painted sky appeared in dozens of films
it was perfect in many ways
but the clouds never moved

"would you like to stop now?"

"yes"

sleepy ear to lawn . . .

I'm listening to the grass
growing under the song

of the approaching mower

Blank Page Already Black

to write is to bring
night into the house

darkness
when fingers
reach the wall

in hand a cave
crawlspace
within the curved palm
enclosed by digits
to dream of a pencil
while fire talks to children

sky the billboard's frame
touches my head
letters scattered to remember
the page is an overgrown forest

forensic first words
climb inside their sounds
shining suits of armor follow
a trail of echoes
through night branches

lost voyage
in seasons spinning

arm over sentence
overhead
not one word at a time
but cluster's imprint
if language then wires

buried in a cramp
the outside wall within
turned to tissue by naming

we are made of
what we are observing

blank page already black

centuries written
over each other in the dark
I could see it better
if I weren't in it

erased space to breathe
in sleep I float
an arm down stream
syllables in the sky conspire

thoughts are animals
that cast no shadow

Farther

walk she said
farther into the hinterland
with a flashlight

dead bark old pages
shadow-stretched branches
twist in the white beam

a passing thought
shivers leaves
pulling a twig
across an albino moon

the sound of a pen writing
on the flesh of an egg
the forest erect with letters
dark script stitching sky to earth

the cryptic signature
of each thing in itself
cast upon the waves
swirling patterns
above as below

walk she said
farther into the night

On the Periphery

The distinctions of what one does
And what is done to him blurs

—George Oppen
Alpine

1

seeing past

a slit in day's side
tunnel through a blackout

conjuring up space

metals rehearse moonlight

life among the targets
dipped in ink
at the center

where nothing returns

2

ingesting the orange horizon
like a hemorrhage
the numbness spreads
from foot to head

body to fill
a spot

26

on the periphery
the dot
that learned to crawl

(speech infection)
every third word
from the sun

I am walking
I am walking

out of my skin

3

leaving a body
paralyzed on the road
in bed in a car
at the beach

hovering over a puppet-self
(staring into his little
wooden eyes)

wake up

4

images peel
off the sentence in strips
seen later as clouds

morphing over a vast
body of water

boundless ocean
on the breath
of a sudden mood swing

the sound of inconsistencies
breaking up on the rocks
scattered pieces
of a gone world in waves

veils of water rise
from the surface like people
evaporating into mist

I am one of them

5

once thought
I am reversed
through condensing rain

weightless on the edge
of a turning circle

always a different opposite
so letters fall from a great height
through holes in the body

hands boil over with words
until at a loss to fill the vast
space of each moment

silence absorbs the landscape

but isn't silent

Sight Lines

                    tightening into

rods and cones
the landscape collapses back on

                    the eye

        (whispered warnings)
        that which
        unseen becomes

                the thing itself

    a thicket of markings
            cancels out
            this passage

                a way of homing

                        the paradox

            where words and things
    conspire in the undergrowth

        so as to prove that writing
                    over writing
                    becomes you

so that when retraced
            the scribbles and cross outs
        assume a signature

"alive" in the socially coded empties
that masquerade as atoms of self

let microscopes adjust us

increased magnification
to weeds and vines

or how I became a moving field

the sky disappears into its color
the texture of

the long return

only in retrospect
do shapes form a life

become the stories we tell ourselves
after the animal

has left its shell

The Gaze

(inside a sideways glance)
passage to the outside
as if this . . .
tunnel were a switch

drifting through matter
where the big shadows roam
a moment before thought
reaches its destination

clear waters carrying a time
her head falls
below the horizon line
a portion of sleep
rubs against the firmament

(disconnect the dots)

at the corners of a room
penciled-in history this
holding still
till the mood shifts

ripples in the present
the feel of words
lifting off
certain objects and people

the phrase "her skin"
rising from columns of numbers

telepathic transference
at the center of a storm

(keep still)

she is growing by subtractions

Write What I Say

write what I say

said someone face over
water in the weeds

drown the instant in ink
flickering eyelight to eros
walk your shadow across the wall

a small red ball hangs from a string

the naked woman in the window
steps behind the curtain

"I've been running in place all my life"
sneers a fat man on tv

an empty train pulls into the station
enter with the others and stare
at the smudged glass

write what I say

~

flesh-dwelling memories
caught in a lover's mandibles
or carved
into a bird-lit tree stump

languorously finger-writing
her name on the window
while we circle the runway

down we go

~

scribbling on the underside
of night (the little hairs
that go unnoticed)

the reticular residue
of dead skin and ash
stains at the bottom of the cup
talk in riddles
dream in code

awaken
with the outward manifestations
of a displaced metaphor
poised at the eye

a photo of the last of her
sitting at a fountain
the relaxed angle of her arm
on cold stone

write what I say

~

emptiness folds into itself
giving birth

(parentheses vibrating)

a man's exhausted
habit-swollen face
on a stalled train of thought
our eyes lock and load

lock and load

~

where the words lead and then
abandon us . . .

like the scent of our own flesh
that's always too much
and not enough

like the sea gull fallen
between parked cars
her motionless eye staring
at no one in particular

like the man on the train
who stands and apologizes
before shooting into the crowd

like the coyote trapped
and gnawing off its foot

like your tongue tracing
the ridges and valleys
of your lover's scars

that's not what I meant

winced the sole survivor
of the burning 747

write what I say

Deader Than Dead

deader than dead
the minuses plus themselves
return to the living in lost numbers
without memory of former lives
or reasons why this one

squeeze through the narrow
underbelly of death's mirror
and out through a trick door
in the reflection of madam's
shiny high heel

across the river in a boat
of match sticks that ignites
at the drop of a perfect number

spreading yourself thinner than one
the zero that erases the board
is already inside waiting
to seed the distant hills

Close Up and Far Away

1

details drain
little lights into people

now and at the hour of our recycling

rain grows upwards
in trails of transparent veins
that cool and cluster into floating cities

the earth shadowed by thoughts

thoughts shadowed by people

people shadowed by machines

sift through image and out
via holographic gill slits

wrapped herself in white noise
and jumped lives at the interface

watched highwaymen haunt the global-grid
and cybersharks track
virtual branchings at the borders

"shall I walk into the flames
or lie down with the numbers
that count me"

2

to be
found out in a crowd

foreign face print
(roll over and play empty)

sweating bullets into the mike
another glassy smile

reading destiny off the cue cards
she admits to everything in principle
but nothing in particular

the court orders a change of mind

swollen dots along the cortex
indicate the path of incision

(when the particle jumps
can we be far behind)

3

"not-knowing
has forced my foot"
stumble forward step . . .

watched herself divide
into two strangers

secret favorite
and *forbidden outcast*

the push-pull
of desire's constant refocusing
endless angles on
planning to arrive . . .

(at the center of every somewhere
there's a road to nowhere)

"I know what you're thinking"
says the psychic holding your keys

"life is much easier now
cleaner more efficient"
says the ceo
to his downsized work force

a forest ranger waves to the car
"in the future we'll talk to the animals
just like I'm talking to you"

4

(something's been erased
but I've forgotten what it was)

"there is no present . . .
enlightenment is in the packaging"
whispers a commodities trader

"rehabilitation can take many lifetimes"
states a 12 step program

"step up to the mike
and tell us about your addiction"
urges the group leader

(reverb screech)

"I *have* . . . talked to the animals
and they're not happy"

"not happy?"

(sparrows chirp overhead)
the cause celeb winks at the camera

"be rest assured
all our animals are happy"

(canned laughter loud enough
to wake the dead)

II

"The pain of the cure is the cure?"

—Richard Foreman
Kate from *The Cure*

The Surgeon's Glove

pressed against the glass
   outlining villages through
                    THIS

(the artificial)

        hand

the size of a mountain
    (officially a closed book)

rivers

the floor washed remains
of a little light

at the crack of a window
or eyelid

where you find yourself

(a moving parenthesis)

blaze of hair

SPLICED

into footage of a golden carp sliding
off the dissecting table

you are turned by another page
(vital signs closely monitored)

the SURGEON

introduces himself
as a count
and opens his umbrella

his face
has been erased

(the curtain rises)

masked lab technicians

moon-walk the gray
tile floor
counting heads
(group movement)

IS THIS AN EMERGENCY
or a lost language

inspired diversions repelling
cliffs as dancing nurses with needles
draw near

memory
(A STATE)

what stands-in-for
takes over

the dream-pendulum
at her door

ancient threshold
at the edge of anesthesia

river in the gutter
where the stick-ships flow

a patient

   discovered
      in a waistcoat
      of iron filings

(star-grained wilderness)

         asleep
        on a hill
        of doorways

   washed up on the front lawn
   of the mayor's mansion

has your life

       grown
       regressed
       cashed in
       jumped ship
       dressed up
       or trickled down

wheeling her into x-ray

(surgeon in the mirror
stretching a rubber glove
over his hand)

sperm-tracers

this is all a mistake

random bits of circumstance
between
the almost never was

and the never again
to be

under the sign
   of the SURGEON-PATIENT

      fused by the scalpel
        connected
        by a thread

              theseus tunneling
         through a cave of ribs
          oven of meditations
           where the subject

   disappears
   in the works

      a cone of light

      small red stone

  unmistakable drift
    into the flesh
of the PATIENT-SURGEON

     operating on himself

(SPOTLIGHT)

> broken letters
> on the sidewalk

clues in the menu

(tongue in the ear)

the search for a second opinion

suspicion:

> vowels open doors

> that consonants
> close

approaching weightlessness
aprés certitude-surgery

watching

the homing arc of a foot (hers)
losing its grip

(HIGH TENSION WIRE)

broken
path to the perimeters
of a secret

turning

back through darkness

few lights

doctors dressed in terminal-codes

seal off
the edges of a life
from its mysteries

silent
journey through the blades

a fan of fingers
segments the horizon

(units of measurement
or characters in a drama)

what is human

mountains straightened
into hospital corners

vivisections of sunlight
on a gray tile floor

her sudden joy in the lightness
of a plastic spoon

tulips (this vase of FEVERS)
exiled from the earth
to dream again
inside a quiet room

a sheet talking to the wind

III

if he heard a voice if only that if he had ever heard a voice voices
if only I had asked him, that I couldn't I hadn't heard it yet the voice
the voices no knowing surely not.

—Samuel Beckett
How it is

Transparencies

deep motored sleep
(roll down the window a scar)

the century was forever ending

spectacle as experience
replayed over anticipation loops

multiple futures keep pointing back
keyed through a screen of possibilities

pick a card

an ocean tracing waves
over beached pages
rewriting early entries
engrained in sand

the sentence took a wrong turn
which made all the difference

the shore line kept changing
a shape eaten by other shapes

there is chaos at the interface

where we left you to yourself
captured by the presence of a crime
to which you keep returning

signature of the abyss
inside each disclosure

transparency lies
at the center

as far as the eye can see

Glass River Divide

day's repair in words
stitching torn sheets of sky
pubescent moon rising

taste of darkened clouds
blotting vermilion streaks
mind marbled
and turning on a spit

bite the terror or release
hesitation at the opening
of the body as threshold

silhouette of my arm
black corridor tilted
to the lower left corner
of a triangular garden

a finger points to a room
the size of an apple
entering through a worm hole
tiny machines holding up the firmament

atoms approach
the great divide
splitting hairs to coax
the animal from its alphabet

pieces of the creature
appear in the guise
of small surface truths
twisting out of reach

face fragments as a puzzle
play desire on a tooth
the other side of identity
comes up heads

multiples pressed into service
parallel functions of appearing
depersonalization attacks
as copies begin bumping into walls

derailed on a train
of thought words whiz
backward like disappearing
cows and trees

matter bent by speed
cleaves to trance notes
short bursts and broken arcs
left as markers in the skin

momentary rip in the facade
exposing
an infinity of false endings
floating toward you in a bottle

Slice of Life

start with the words

ceremony

at the center
of a disturbance

season of spare parts

(to have stared at the same stain
for 15 years)

to open the cover of a book and find
a miniature author inside

asleep in his coffin

the child
dressed as a ghost
carries a rubber hatchet

words attach themselves
to his eyes

the world won't let go

days dismembered by memory

is this the language sought
or just another

inherited gesture

a way of signaling
in advance

the cop teaches his club a new twist

the irate consumer clicks his remote control

the doctor depresses your tongue with a stick

the detective bares his teeth at the neighbor's dog

the actress masturbates in her mirror

the assassin locks-in on the candidate

who's inside whom

ghosts in the bones

you could have fooled
my camera

every slipped desire
quietly cutting

the air into pieces

like some deranged fan

The Mirror and Its Double

While passing a dimly lit café, I saw my double again for a moment
behind the bar; my fear was too tenuous to make me start, my start-
ing to be noticeable—I just went on

—Peter Handke
The Weight of the World

to place your head upon a plate
and hear the sharpening
of knives in the background

thrown back upon
the face of the double
in chalk we dream

free floating parallel lines
swim breath beside you
borrowing an ear

lost secrets live echoes
particle-currents in the veins
whispers while you write

moist earth buried in the body
of answers say circular ruins
peeling back the skin

or turning a page
landscape with friends standing
on a hill of yellow leaves

that which seeing itself
steps outside and stares back
at the stranger you have become

he who shadows your steps
your desire to see
through the eyes of the dead

the future ghost inside you
projected outward
as a silent doppleganger

your reflection on the window
the face that reads you backwards
spreads its glassy features over the river

words are only the tips of waves

Fractal Geometry

the sea dreams
of a ship
the paper
a pen

cross the expanse
the limits
heard as echoes off
a far shore

observing events
as windowless monads
as mirrors flashing
through a field of signs
(I am standing
between the arrows)

exploded cell
outward into darkness
(brain loop burning)

once the sun
now a spreading
circumference of thought
pinpoints this
alphabetical displacement

misreadings create
new voyages

voices in our ears
back from the periphery
widow forth a tune

Marginalia

> We are whole edges.
> If I turn to sleep
> the same will urge tomorrow.
> There are no capsule versions.
> The crystals are the wall.

—Clark Coolidge
The Crystal Text

what provokes this shrinking
in from the margins

(a crow's peck
punctuating the red zone)

approaching history via simulation
a quarry of ribs
questions the limits of sand

what's found
(soon forgotten)

the past was never
quite present

~

small
grammatical spasms
linked to intestinal gurglings

a body murmurs
through the granulated "I"

about a family photo under glass
from which it is trying
to awaken

~

our lips
still joined by cinematic scar tissue
chase distances between
dizzy cross-stepping

man in a torn red uniform
motions from the movie marquee
(the smile has begun
to smear on his face)

~

stroking your throat
under the bridge

shining eyes cut into the world
at the crossroads
(your head turns the house
counter clock-wise)

facelettes of the moon
collecting on an empty plate

a pecking of heels disappears
down a stone courtyard

~

observer of a giant-speck
moving between magnifications
(the insect's roving antennae)

shadow of a plane
across rows of abandoned buildings

"why have you come here"

(silence)

turn your head

dark smudge on the wall

(the world begins again
without notice)

Little Numbers

If you ask me what time is,
I don't know the answer.
If you don't ask me, I do.

—St. Augustine

and the walls fall
into each other
as lover's flesh
sticks to the shape
of certain numbers

water talks to the pond
to here and nowhere
drips response repose

5 8 13 embedded
in the bulrushes
quiver and hum

how the magnified point
spreads into a field
and the spaces sing

little numbers
little numbers

who can hold you
without crumbling

Empty When We Look

menu the heart
in successive stages

little white flags
pinned on the pain
serve as burial sites

swollen rivers spill
syllables over the rocks
in overheard streams

raise the roof inside her palm

a puppet's ladder to the moon
lands on a child's bed

foot upon a rung of sky

begin to disappear

with each step

~

the shape of becoming

nothing

unfinished to the end
palimpsest of the waves

corresponding to the littoral shore
curled inside the crook
of a dreaming cartographer's arm

~

a horse is not a house

the flutter of translations
settles into indirection
more presence than shape

vapors collect
around the moving edges
of a missing person

~

identity grows another
set of eyes

landscape injections
fill in the background
with replaceable parts

(let's go to the image bank)

slow motion paradox
in the tissues
coughs up blood

~

mirror of no return
torn phrases and misplaced limbs
tango across her eyes

pressed into film
her shadow walks
through rows of archways

damaged light
settles on the dust

~

walls pull back and dissolve
into dozens of roads spinning
from her head like braided wires

searching the prism of ground stones
for a spark
to uncover the beyond by digging

to find nothing
but not see it
to become buried in a name

where the words stop
she is not she

in the exactitude of uncertainty
she is what does not stop

The Rapture

"How could an argument soothe or settle a controversy, when every
word is a nest for a bird of doubt?"

—Edmond Jabès
The Book of Questions

black harvest of holes
ladder of pre-speak

face mapped in mumbled streets
wire crossings at the cheeks
and forehead a foot
with no place to rest

blue spotted haze (meaning)
the hills in his eyes

distance drawn
between the edges
never to be traversed

a hand cut off at the gesture
suspended in space

edible darkness
stirs in the marrow

the mouth opens
and closes

opens and closes

~

71

stanzas erase us
as soon as they are written

eyes roll back
bending him into pliant rivers
unfolding night features
a voice behind his left ear

this is the phrasal footpath
an island named fire
and a human skeleton
wearing the head of a fish

~

wordy tissue collecting
in the corridors
(yellowed paper)

writing on the inside
of this moment's coffin

what's nailed down
dreams of being pried up
planted in air

wingspan
of a solitary moment
passing through the page

the road floating overhead
appears lifetimes away

~

flattened vista
on the face of the next

stranger

when he finally turns his head
the sun goes down

times table two
close one eye
(the spot keeps returning)

the inevitable payback
days waiting
for the philosopher's stool

(lift photo)
marked cards moving
letters under image

if pain persists
see a professional

~

awake inside the materials

each step a falling into
held together by
ropes and pulleys

inhabiting the voice
then gestures
the wood that forms a face

the x'd out calendar
little nervous twitches
that turn into one big tick

filling in the negative outline
of a head

a single stick of light
pokes the debris
(as per instructions)

73

~

curling his lips back
in the hotel mirror

this is your history
drawn upon the face
of a playing card
(who's playing you)

the narrows responded in kind
ocean's imprint
on found fragments

a few rounded and fused
stones in his pocket
holding him to earth

to grow old
but never be released
from the rapture
the road on which
we finally lay our heads

IV

"No one else could ever be admitted here, since this gate was made only for you. I am now going to close it."

—Franz Kafka
Before the Law

Orpheus Dividing

1

in autumn
fallen
out of time

slow syllables
passing through flesh
(how he sees himself
chipped from words)

marble hand
lying in the leaves

tipped ladders into darkness
the analytic mind
lowered on a rope

eyes fluttering behind stone lids
the rustle of pigeons
perched
on a sill

(he who escapes with his head)

2

nocturnal park surrounding
the thought of when
he was a statue
now an image
to be digitally
recombined with others

clouds cast
a sidereal edge
near a photo of
his severed hand

five stolen fingers
five steps across the strings
the unit of time taken

(walking out of himself)

eurydice's radioactive footprints
through the parking lot
through the fairgrounds
and shopping mall

through the miniature golf course
and into the woods

3

music's blindfold

eye of memory slow scanning
SMALL TOWN AMERICA in caps
(look again)

victorian columns and village greens
sleepy lakes decoded and dripping
disappear and regroup
into spliced sentiments
cut-up tv heads
real life dramas jingles
and slogans

pieces of pop tunes hum us
the hours grow ears
noise is misspelled music

a displaced motor irritates
an idea inside the shell
the confused character
muffles a cough

(eurydice where are you)

meaning as both disease and cure
mirror and pit
a boat across the waves
and the bottomless sea itself

4

static inside
certain idioms

to be where he is not

scanned and duplicated
at the onset

morphing personality modifications
to click on traits

(operation cyborg city)
proceed with extreme prejudice

assumes the position
becomes a terminal
with portable mindscreen
and electronic entrails

the body is vestigial
all pleasures vicarious

welcome to the virtual community

5

talking to the dead on a floppy disk
(insert graphics)

hologram of orpheus' head
watching himself
falter and forget

divided down to his cells
by tireless maenads
music is misspelled noise
(this is not his hand)

blood pressure descending
into the underworld

lack of pulse
troubleshooting
on/off protocol d-i-p switch

6

wormholes in the machine

nested inside nests
inside the circuitry

(eurydice's eyes)

cancel unprinted text
reversed through a funnel of coordinates
a series of instants forced
inside out

while the exterior
is injected within

afterlife in information

the bloated body of

transparent desires

useless hands and feet

stretched across the landscape

7

identity in the materials
tip of a finger

pixellated geography
tracks intersecting the surrounding
panoply of signs

hardware handshake
her lips for a moment
on another channel

(to be awake inside language)
rate of insertion point

*   blinking   *

back from the dead
(interface instructions)

desire born from division
forgets the message
turning back to find
an empty dress caught
in the branches of a rose bush

"we've lost her"

"go to commercial"

a chorus of slashed zeros
(alive in the circuitry)
kick-two-three-four

the curtains begin to close

oh orpheus

lever (alarm) locking disk

random access memory
replaying his severed head
still singing

across rivers
of flickering screens

V

What difference does it make who is speaking?

—Michel Foucault
What Is an Author?

The French Disease

aprés le déluge
you write stolen sentences
on my arms and legs
so I can pass for fiction

the french disease
is injected into the alphabet
as a vaccine against nausea
and multiple misreadings

squirm in nuance
and talk on the tips of waves
(take two of these . . .
and see me in your dreams)

big-time producers take no prisoners
(schizophrenia seems
a plus in these parts)
the jungle inches forward
the moment you look away

elevator music soothes
the savage writer
connect the bones and the sound bites
flow through my tears
(you originals are the biggest dupes)

then someone dies
with his hands in his pockets
and a shark ups the ante
he who is left in mystery
counting his guitar strings

tv produces glowing afterlife
in the corners of the couch
(who put that pod in my closet)
"I know what you're going through"
she whispered
over a loudspeaker in the park
driving into the sunset
the motel signs all call me by name

what country past dreams etc.
or locomotive in the skull
has not been imagined and forgotten
only to be drummed up again
in fragments as glimpses
of a fabled city resting
on the head of a pin

bubbles burst
and worlds split into multiples
come up on the big screen
as quantum foam

a fluidity of angles
mirroring the simulacra among us
that distort every essence
pointing to different roads taken
by other you's

glass shards in the skin
like knives dividing the instants
whose instants

("I'm not involved here" she thinks
but is captured by the reverb)

Intimacy

There are two men without feet, they are tall men
swimming through matter.

—Kathleen Fraser
Wing, IX. Matter

a creaking curtain rises on wooden legs
halting two feet above the stage
where an italian foot-play begins . . .

picking quantum from her hair

"this is where they hide the light"

(her first third-person reaction
seemed fresher this time)

"the shore line is closer now
your face larger
than the nearest mountain"

a clutch of women
with lit candles in their mouths
comes closer
handing her a notebook

"spit on the fire
and become the flame"

(language returned her to herself
only when she wasn't thinking)

87

the story recedes slowly
leaving letters on the carpet
and clustered mumbles along the hairline

a mental foreshortening
words pressed into a kind of paste
the consistency of crushed
insects in matted hair
plus years of attitude
gumming up the works

(but the words can't plug up the holes
because the holes are in the words)

the walls tilt
toward the center of the room
and the furniture
begins to slide

a large red O glides
through the window on a string

suddenly breaking out a deck of cards
"perhaps you're not dreaming this . . .

perhaps your left hand
being fashioned from venetian glass
and placed upon her right
shoulder might . . ."

an elbow pokes into the frame

"remember me? remember me?"
(close smell of cold sweat)
"I'm the one who loves you
but I died"

open-eyed or blindfolded
ready or not
the personal pronoun

goes down with the ship
(as is the custom in these parts)

"who isn't memory's creation"
the curtain's broken legs
slowly descend

freckled twins
facing a high mirror
slowly turn their heads
to the audience in unison

and smiling present their
mirror-doubles
as more perfect selves

State of Mind

inside the institute of barking codes
clock ticking slumber streets
margin of image control

stripped to examine
tighten command modules
(learning to dream by the numbers)

orange clouds circle back as breath
congestion in the main arteries

organs or government buildings
body of signs flashing
across 10 million screens

invisible limbs linked
to multiple terminals
a cybernetic forest
of extended egos

image splicing
personality types for reentry
rerouting neurons
to signal words
(we're in the wiring)

hundreds of re-borns
slowly milling at the mall

Dream of the Everyday World

boy in a photo pointing
at the sun. . .

(memory of my head above water
drifting downstream)

speaking in a forgotten tongue
a writer enters the creaking
joints of language
(old melody of loose parts)

bending light off opaque surfaces
shapes moving in the ripples
peck at him
whispering sudden doubts

(fear burns at the fibers of a rope
just out of reach)

crawling deeper into the quotidian
where hidden attractors
transform domestic repetitions
into meditations on a spoon

a mother picks up
her child's propeller plane
and recalls her first night of love

an old woman descending a staircase
sees herself stepping
in front of a moving train

the patient keeps time
by banging his head against the wall

the man tapping at the window
wants to read your meter

to dispel rumors of divorce
the guests fake orgasm
while their hosts listen in the next room

the local wise guy's head
is held underwater
till he finally stops kicking
and sees *the light*

staring into a bowl of green jello
the student wonders
(will having an affair with you
make her boyfriend jealous)

the jogger in the park
eyes the bushes and imagines
hairy hands stretching out
to snatch her

the balding gynecologist
snaps off his rubber gloves
thinking of a balloon rising
with his wife clutching
the end of the rope

past the point of letting go
she floats headfirst
into the mouth
of a hovering ufo

Nobody

numbered face the floating orb
skull past features
shrunken asteroid heart
orbiting a light bulb

precarious seed
red hours round
a house on alert
growing arms and legs

sun at ground zero
follows eye off horizon
line of least resistance
split into black 9s and 6s

stirred by rhythm's focus
forget-me-not head on a wire
flowering filigree of yes and no
the you in unstable atoms

impacted 8 in the jawbone
dissolves the woods into lines and swirls
fever at the crossroads
forms a face

chipped away by day
several 2s and 3s uncovered
in the nose and cheek
smell of damp earth under skin

alive and counting
heads in the park
pages of an anatomy book
pulled apart by the wind

That

that draws itself inside a hole
the walls stuffed with newspaper
and torn clothing an argument
addressed to an insect

that is ill at ease dizzy detached
a stranger inside her skin
guilty as the offending letter
in a misspelled word

that won't sleep straight but twists
turning gets up and crawls on all fours
speaks in short bursts punctuated
by twitches and tics

that tunnels under the house
to store the evidence of a lifetime
in paper bags and boxes

that cools his heels with grass-lined shoes
that keeps a stick for snakes and dogs

that sees animals in human faces
that sports stolen shades
that kicks out in her dreams

that shits his pants
that eats from the corner's cage
that knifes someone in his sleep

that pushes a shopping cart
that bites   that moans
that grabs and clings
that claws   that clutches

that burrows and buries
her tongue in the grave
of his mouth

Hauling Light Home in a Box

in memory of Breton's Nadja

thoughts enter unseen
through a wormhole in the skull
the dimensions of a city
very much like this one

skin rubbed into a fine powder
to close the book on
to write across steamed glass
so as to glimpse
her face in the markings

the slender volume of her arm
slung over the driver's seat
like light whispering to the foreground

get in . . .

the engine turns over
chance alchemy of loose parts
unleashed upon the open road

to see your own madness
in the next seat
placing her hand over your eyes
and pressing down on the pedal

flung free from body-earth
driving blind
through a turn of phrase
into the outstretched arms of the void

memory of the moment before
you pulled her hand from your eyes
you were
on fire

luminous as a letter
ubiquitous as dust

Second Sight

who is (nobody thinks)
a caged mask
see pictures reconstructed moments
building a womb
inside language

rest a finger on the blade
something rubs the earth open
lifting the lid
of the corpse
the pupil
still floating on a milky lake

transparent
film of self sliding over surface
perception in the act of
appearing
little orphan random
rolls the dice

the eye that sees through me
the I that escapes
through a hole in the subject
disappearing into daylight
over-exposed landscape
liquid formed sleep
in a drop
reduced to dots on a map

two steps across
the field in a shadow
the season's yellowed hands
sequential stirrings

from root to stem
joined at the letters

as the worm is my witness
he who has crawled
out of the ruins of his skin
leaving a molted suit
on the seat next to him

crossing the a.m.
damp leaves the left side
of the sentence overturned
in object revolt if I
had a hammer defense against
the bottom line (weather permitting)

rumble of furniture in the firmament
throwing dirt into an open mouth
the other side of now
where all the drowned pictures go

Eye to Eye

word wandering ship
the consistency of clouds
small flame
at the end of a finger

cannibal sun
inching above the tall grasses
stories in the melting wax
the transported self scattered

driftwood on the beach
see through me
where we walked
stone lit for days

if birds
say flight or forget
one bell on a branch
swept the fallen
pieces into piles

where the house finds me
where my eyes have rolled

the dog on the ceiling
doesn't see me
so the letters form teeth
and the sentence barks

tiny buzzing needles
sew words into flesh

drawn from a patchwork of signs
a floating hat and burning cigar
an open umbrella

wash of sea and sky
through her transparent body

what's left assumes
the shape of absence

as if here
were no longer a local matter

Code Heroes

he screwed on his motorized hands
and moved the metallic digits

a wrrrring glitch in the background
made the words indecipherable

as the doctor dozed at his desk
two 12 inch phantoms approached

every object hides that part of the world
which stands immediately behind it

the marks on her neck
matched his dental work

the twins climbed out of the pool "I am your reflection"
said the first "I am truth reflected" said the second

gazing into the infinity between her lips and eyes
he realized he was remembering a perfume ad

the crowd let out a long "ouuuuu"
when the man on the roof wavered in the wind

the unfolded map
was unreadable at the creases

she said they couldn't go on lying to each other
he said he thought they could "no problem"

only when the train doors closed
did we realize we were going in the wrong direction

"you said you were watchin' but you weren't
now look what happened!"

"listen jimmy just 'cause superman sees through things
doesn't mean he understands them"

a beatific smile spread over the mechanic's face
"sure I can fix it . . . but it'll cost ya"

he took the poem by the shirt and shook it
(start with a fight and end up dancing)

at the eye of the whirlpool there is only the movement
of the water (the vortex n'existe pas)

a mother's fears baked into a pie so nice
and warm (eat and become one of us)

knowing their buttons were being pushed
didn't stop the audience's tears from flowing

as soon as she started talking about her problems
the analyst announced the session was over

the pop icon said "repetition is a form of originality
since you can't drink the same coke twice"

"for me" sneered the cop "the chalk drawing
has become more interesting than the dead body"

in the intersection he had become a pedestrian
but once on the other side he was a doctor again

"this is my body" said the cyborg
being lowered into a vat of bubbling acid

circle the word that best describes your disposition
A) friendly B) helpful C) gregarious D) sarcastic
E) vengeful

wise in the ways of the code
she never returned his calls

Acquired Characteristics

blind man rocking
circles on a watch
leave the revolution meter running
muzzle wrench enforcer
and her faithful dog roar-shock

deactivate abstraction-divider
as implement of terror
crossed wires
predictably hedging all bets
pretender reigns
tupperware dialectics
take one and see

angry brains bursting through the hairline
addressing the regulars as natives
pop-tart ethics I read it on a box
step lively when finally chosen
pointing to the map
this is my nation's landfill
I shall not want

open and say ahhhh . . .
perimeters of the problem
this yoke of sincerity
spotlight on: *my trampled feelings*
another backyard tragedy
complete with trimmings

blind-sided rhythm shot in the act of
these hands want more
a seizure of events beyond our control
these self-reflexive straitjackets

come in various sizes
techniques for reducing stress
can I rent you my paranoia
antagonistic adenoids
refuse to talk to strangers
memory is as memory does

chalk-marked quotidian
fire in the garden of forms
someone becomes her words
as soon as they are written

twilight of the grammarians
my lower left bicuspid
doesn't live here anymore
so what to make of all these childhood ruins

victims of the vicarious
no time to rolodex their dreams
I can almost see
the big "E" she thinks
no one's old enough to die
most times the point
just gets in the way

Severed Moon

severed moon rising

through charts and alphabets
our senses buried
in the tools of measurement

rent in the fabric
the torn tapestry of our remains

in the mountains there are shoulders
striations map the rock
undersigned by centuries

the automatic among us
traveling at rem-speed
collision course of variables

diversions drawn out
disassembling the moving point
into a series of choking sensations

what gets through
a residue of longing
circling a life by degrees

still water between ripples
another way of saying

put your ear against
the nothing within

the hypnotic pull of the target
atomic bull's-eye
inside the black hole of writing

open mouth
flowing through the stops
legs walking washed
alive among forms

flattening angles and fleeting vistas
landscape reduced to a line
to climb out on a few words
before the branch breaks

angle of approach
in echoes off the rocks
artifice of attraction
insomnia's trickster-god
reads us the law of reversals

hyphenated-laughter
adrift in darkness
quartermaster to the hanged moon
second skin of light
over the face of the lake

brain-dead
but the mouth keeps talking